Liberal
Fascism

by Micky Barnetti

DEDICATION

This book is dedicated to all victims of fascism,
including those in the past and those tomorrow morning
and each morning thereafter.

Anarchists say:
"What students in government schools (fascist schools)
are NOT taught would fill a book."

Here it is.

CONTENTS

ACKNOWLEDGMENTS

This book is the handiwork of the Dead Writers Club (DWC). Please direct complaints accordingly. The Pointer Institute deserves special thanks for "pointing out" many improvements. DWC is thankful for the ongoing assistance of No Pledge Publishing.

- 1 -

EVERYTHING YOU KNOW
ABOUT FASCISM IS WRONG

Francis Bellamy claimed that he authored the Pledge of Allegiance. It is clear that he participated in authoring the program (spanning two newspaper pages) that contained the original Pledge of Allegiance.

Most students are taught lies about Bellamy, although most states have laws mandating that every school begin each day with the modern version of Bellamy's Pledge of Allegiance. Why are students kept in the dark about Bellamy and the daily ritual?

There are shocking reasons why schools will not educate students about Bellamy and the pledge's past. Many old shockers (Bellamy's Christian Socialism) have been supplemented by new shockers uncovered by the preeminent authority Dr. Rex Curry. This book explains the old along with these jaw-dropping new discoveries, including:

(1) The Pledge of Allegiance was the origin of the Fascist salute and Fascist behavior.

(2) The Fascist salute came from the military salute due to the use of the military salute in the original Pledge of Allegiance.

The dogma that Bellamy touted (socialism) had global impact and led to additional new discoveries by Dr. Curry, to wit:

(3) The Swastika, although an ancient symbol, was also used to represent crossed "S" letters for "socialism" under Adolf Hitler's National Socialist German Workers Party (Nazis).

(4) Hitler transformed his own signature to appear as a stylized "S" letter reflecting the design of his swastika symbol and his dogma of socialism.

Another discovery revealed by this book is the widespread ignorance about the revelations enumerated above.

There are many books about Hitler, or Fascists, or the Pledge of Allegiance. Every book about Hitler, Fascists, or the pledge reveals that the book's authors overlooked all the disclosures enumerated above. How were those writers blind to the preceding discoveries? Their ignorance spans more than a century (if the years are counted from 1892, the year that Bellamy's pledge was published), or it spans more than half a century (if the years are counted since World War II and Hitler's reign).

Many people (including "scholars") have written about Hitler's Schutzstaffel (the "SS Division") and its stylized "SS" symbol. Some authors have noted that the "SS" symbol uses runes that correspond to the letter "S" as alphabetical symbolism for the word "Schutzstaffel." All of those authors failed to compare the "SS" symbol to the swastika symbol, and failed to discover the alphabetical symbolism of the swastika for "socialism" under Hitler.

Why did it take so long to uncover the facts enumerated in this book? And why do news outlets continue to perpetuate ignorance about the Pledge of Allegiance and about this exposé?

One explanation for the ignorance is: government schools (socialist schools) will not teach the truth about Francis Bellamy and the Pledge of Allegiance. Bellamy abetted those two major hallmarks of the police state in the United States (hereafter the "USA") and its constant growth: (1) Government (socialist) schools; (2) The Pledge of Allegiance.

Bellamy wanted government to take over schools. Bellamy achieved "equality" by making everyone equally stupid via government schools. Government's schools are never going to tell the truth about him and his pledge. If they taught the truth, then no one would perform the pledge (other than weirdos).

The pledge represents a threat of violence. People were persecuted, beaten, jailed, and lynched for defying the pledge in the similar rituals in the USA, German, and worldwide. The pledge continues to inspire bullying and persecution. The topic intimidates journalists as it has intimidated so many other people.

News Journalists remain too brainwashed and frightened to inform their readers. Their news outlets will not publish photographs or film recordings of the early pledge's Nazi salute. They will not write about what the photos and films show.

Experiments were performed in which news reporters were asked to publish photographs and films of the early pledge salute and to examine its influence on Germany and other countries. All of the journalists refused.

The same journalists were accused of being dishonest cowards. They continued to refuse any coverage of the issues in this book. Of those same journalists, none disputed the conclusions in this book. The experiment has also been performed by the Pointer Institute for Media Studies. Anyone can replicate the experiment.

All of the above is more proof that the USA is a police state. Journalists demonstrate that the pledge is effective obedience training. They lack understanding of private property rights, supply-and-demand pricing, laissez-faire economics, free markets, individual rights, and capitalism. Twelve years of Bellamy's schools prevent newspapers, TV, and radio outlets from telling the truth. Instead, reporters spend their careers glorifying lies from public officials. It is Stockholm Syndrome. Bellamy's scheme worked.

That is why government schools are unconstitutional: They violate the First Amendment right to freedom of speech and freedom of the press. Government schools (socialist schools) tell everyone what to think and say and write. The Pledge of Allegiance is a part of that.

The Bellamy dogma of "Christian Socialism" renders government (socialist) schools unconstitutional as an establishment of religion and as a violation of freedom of religion. Separation of church and state cannot exist where, as in the U.S., the state is your church.

An old cliche states: History is written by the victors. It would be more accurate to state: History is written by the government. In government's schools (socialist schools) the government glorifies itself as a hero, and not as the universal and eternal monster.

Harry Browne, the best-selling author, said that the greatest mistake in history was letting the government educate our children. The historian Dr. Rex Curry said: "Remove the pledge from the flag; remove flags from schools; remove schools from government."

- 2 -

AMERICAN FASCIST FRANCIS BELLAMY

Francis Julius Bellamy (May 18, 1855 to August 28, 1931) was born in Mount Morris, New York; however, his family moved to Rome when Bellamy was five years old. That was the city of Rome in the state of New York (not in Italy).

While in Rome (NY), he was educated at a school known as the "Rome Free Academy" (RFA). The Rome Free Academy continues to operate in Rome, NY. The RFA's school logo includes two fasces symbols.

Bellamy's connection to Rome, NY, is important because it was the origin of the "ancient Roman salute" myth (that the stiff-armed gesture is an ancient gesture from the Roman Empire) that was debunked by Dr. Curry.

Because Bellamy was from Rome, NY, the term "Roman salute" was used to refer to the gesture for Bellamy's Pledge of Allegiance (both the original gestures and the stiff-armed gesture - the classic Nazi salute - that developed from Bellamy's original gestures).

People from the city of Rome in the state of New York were referred to as "Romans" during Bellamy's life (and they continue to refer to themselves as "Romans" today). One example of that is the headline: "Roman Lived to See U.S. Adopt Famed Flag Salute" from the Utica Observer newspaper (August 28, 1936). As time went by, some confused people believed that the "Roman salute" referencing the city in New York, was instead a reference to ancient Rome in Italy.

Bellamy continues to reside in Rome, NY. He is buried in the Rome cemetery.

The early stiff-armed gesture in the USA's Pledge of Allegiance was not an ancient Roman salute. There was no such thing as an "ancient Roman salute" (unless one counts the middle finger salute, mentioned by Suetonius and Martial). The modern Roman salute myth evolved from the USA's Pledge of Allegiance.

Many cities in the state of New York have names reminiscent of classical history (Albany, Ithaca, Syracuse, Troy, and Utica), and that is why New York is the "Empire State" with the "Empire State Building" because it is a reference to the time period of the ancient Roman Empire.

As Bellamy's Nazi salute spread, so spread his government (socialist) schools, and so spread the use of the fasces symbol to represent socialism. The "Rome Free Academy" school that Bellamy attended continues to operate in Rome, New York, and the school's logo includes two fasces. The official seal of the United States Senate (adopted 1886) includes a pair of crossed fasces. Two fasces appear on either side of the flag of the United

States behind the podium in the United States House of Representatives. The fasces style is used in the Lincoln Memorial (the fronts of the chair's arms shaped to resemble fasces). A fasces is on the bronze George Washington statue (1882) in front of Federal Hall National Memorial in Manhattan, New York City. The fasces appears on the U.S. dime from 1916. The fasces style (as a bundle of arrows) adorns the U.S. quarter (1932) and resembles the emblem on the hat worn by Mussolini in a notorious photograph.

Mussolini was so impressed with the Roman and socialist themes in the U.S. that he honored Rome, NY with a statue of the "Capitoline Wolf" (upon which the fabled Romulus and Remus are shown suckling). The peculiar statue stands in front of The Beeches Inn in Rome, NY, where it is adorned with a plaque displaying a fasces and the phrase "New Rome." Mussolini made similar gifts to Cincinnati and to Rome in the state of Georgia (in 1931). An engraving on one of the statues reads "Anno X" ("Year 10" in Latin), referencing Mussolini's tenth year in power.

Mussolini learned the Bellamy salute when he was a powerful socialist leader. No "ancient Roman" influence (real or imagined) was mentioned by Bellamy, nor by James Upham (the person who assisted Bellamy in creating the Pledge's gesture), in their descriptions of how the Pledge and its salute was written.

Francis Bellamy never used the term "ancient Roman salute" when describing his pledge's salute.

The phrase "Roman salute" did not exist at the time that Bellamy and Upham worked on the pledge (Dr.

Curry's work is supported by the Oxford English Dictionary in this etymological regard). The concept of the "ancient Roman salute" was dreamed up decades after Bellamy wrote the pledge of Allegiance.

Francis Bellamy clearly explained that his pledge began with a military salute that was then extended out toward the flag. In practice, the second gesture was performed palm-down with a stiff-arm when the military salute was merely pointed out at the flag by bored children forced to do Bellamy's programmed chanting daily in government schools. That is how the straight-arm salute developed from Francis Bellamy's Pledge of Allegiance and its use of the military salute (and how the USA's pledge salute led to the Nazi salute).

An instructor at George Mason University (GMU) wrote a short item for the American Philological Association questioning whether the so-called "ancient Roman salute" ever occurred in any Roman art or text. The item noted that the salute occurred in early silent films: the American "Ben-Hur" (1907), the Italian "Nerone" (1908), "Spartaco" (1914), and "Cabiria" (1914).

Thereafter, Dr. Curry publicly announced his discovery that the original U.S. flag salute (1892) pre-dated and inspired the use of the gesture in the later films. The pledge's early Nazi salute had been unknown to the GMU instructor when he wrote about the films.

The GMU teacher went on to author a confusing book that was debunked by Dr. Curry before it was published. He does not dispute Dr. Curry's discovery that Pledge of Allegiance was the origin of the Nazi salute and Nazi behavior. GMU's instructor does not state that David's Horatii was the origin of the Roman salute myth. He states that Horatii is the "starting point for an arresting gesture that progressed from oath-taking to what will become known as the Roman salute," which actually states nothing, and is an apparent reference to his own "starting point" for writing his book. He does not contend that the painting was the origin of the Nazi salute, nor that it was the origin of the "ancient Roman salute" myth.

His book seems written to evade any comparison of Bellamy's socialism to the socialism touted by Mussolini and Hitler.

The GMU author was debunked also by Michelle Borg at the University of Sydney: "The author first turns to the early form of the Pledge of Allegiance, which originally included an entirely similar gesture to the one that came to be used by Fascists and Nazis. This uncomfortable association is not explored in depth; [He] simply asserts that the gesture had no political or historical connotations in the United States."

Borg's criticism applies to Wikipedia too, depending on the date and time.

How can anyone ignore more than a century of robotic brainwashing in government schools, boy scouts and girl scouts, modern Olympics, other sporting events, political rallies, parades and more? How does anyone ignore the persecution, bullying, and violence used to dictate the gesture and the mechanical chanting? How is it ignored today?

Fictitious Roman scenes in early silent movies only

added to the "Roman" salute myth that developed from the Pledge of Allegiance (which preceded those films by more than a decade).

That the myth of the "ancient Roman salute" did not exist when Bellamy wrote his pledge (and for decades thereafter) also means that the concept of the "Roman salute" did not even exist when Jacques-Louis David painted his "Oath of the Horatii." Thus David was NOT thinking of a real or imagined "Roman salute" when he painted the Horatii, nor did David ever use the term "Roman salute" (again also see the Oxford English Dictionary).

The Horatii lie (that the Horatii painting was the origin of the "Roman salute" myth) is a very recent lie. It first appeared on Wikipedia (~2006) after Dr. Curry's discovery that the Pledge of Allegiance was the origin of the Nazi salute. Research produces no examples in history of anyone asserting that the Horatii painting was an example of an ancient Roman salute, nor that it inspired the "Roman salute" myth. The Horatii disinformation was deliberately fabricated by a liar to cover-up Dr. Curry's discovery that the pledge was the origin of the Nazi salute, to cover up the pledge's putrid past, and to side-step the influence of American socialists (e.g. Edward Bellamy, Francis Bellamy) and the USA's pledge upon German socialism and socialism worldwide.

In the Horatii painting, three brothers are reaching for weapons (and the two figures in back are reaching with their left hands).

The same liar who created the Horatii deceit had, until he was debunked, previously claimed that the stiff-armed salute was an actual ancient Roman salute, and he posted the lie that Roman statues displaying "adlocutio" (a gesture made by a person speaking) showed "the ancient Roman stiff-armed salute."

Wikipedia continues to mislead readers about the "ancient Roman salute" lie in articles that vary in quality from "confusing" to "deceptive." Liars on Wakipedia are similar to journalists in the old media: They will not write about the pledge's influence on socialism in Germany and elsewhere, and they will delete any information in that regard. They also do not dispute the information in this book (they merely suppress it).

The newly substituted Horatii falsity has been mindlessly repeated by many people (as the adlocutio lie was repeated and still is) because wakipedia glorifies itself as an encyclopedia, even though it is merely an anonymous bulletin board where anyone can post anything.

It should be needless to say (but for wakipedia) that Bellamy was not influenced by Jacques-Louis David's painting "Oath of the Horatii." According to Bellamy, his pledge's gesture resulted when he was with James Upham and Upham specifically suggested gestures for the pledge that Bellamy had penned. Upham suggested the military salute followed by the arm outstretched with the palm upward (which was similar to saying "Here is the flag").

It was the use of the military salute (at the beginning of the original Pledge of Allegiance and then extended outward toward the flag) that resulted in the classic Nazi-style gesture.

From the pledge's breech birth in 1892, the stiff-armed gesture grew in popularity and was used during meetings of fraternal organizations, including the Masons. Bellamy and Upham were Masons and they both specifically promoted the use of the pledge (and its straight-arm salute) by fraternal organizations and by the Masons.

Germans learned American behavior via old films, WWI, news reels, and the widespread use of the straight-arm salute by Germans who had studied or lived in the USA; via Americans who also studied or lived in Germany; via German-American groups in the USA (including the German-American Bund); via the Boy Scouts (who spread both the American Nazi salute and also the swastika symbol); via the official Olympic salute (another exposé by Dr. Curry is that the "official Olympic salute" was the USA's Nazi salute from the Pledge of Allegiance).

From 1892 through 1942, public officials (including U.S. presidents, congressmen, governors, state legislators and everyone down to the local dog catcher) performed the American Nazi salute. In 2015, news outlets reported secret home movie footage from 1933 showing the "Nazi salute" performed by Edward the VIII and the future Queen Elisabeth (at seven years old). No American news reporter was aware that public officials in the USA performed the gesture from 1892 through 1942.

Before WWII, it was not illegal for citizens of the USA to support the National Socialist German Workers' Party or Hitler's political campaigns.

The National Socialist German Workers' Party (NSGWP) began in 1920, achieved electoral breakthroughs in 1930, imposed dictatorship in 1933, and invaded Poland in 1939 as allies with the Union of Soviet Socialist Republics in a pact to divide up Europe, spreading World War II, and leading to the socialist Wholecaust (of which the Holocaust was a part).

The pledge's stiff-armed salute existed from 1892 (three decades before the NSGWP) and continued in the USA throughout the existence of the NSGWP. It was the origin of the Nazi salute.

- 3 -

EDWARD BELLAMY'S FASCISM

Francis Bellamy was cousin and comrade of Edward Bellamy, the author of the internationally best-selling book "Looking Backward" published in 1888. The book spawned "Nationalism" clubs worldwide and both Bellamy boys were self-professed socialists who supported the movement, its "Nationalist" magazine, and the Nationalist Educational Association (NEA) -named to deliberately to mimic the National Education Association (NEA) in the USA.

Francis Bellamy used his position with the National Education Association (NEA) to promote "military socialism" -the dogma that he touted with his cousin. In 1892, Bellamy became chairman of the National Education Association's executive committee for a National Public School Celebration plan that would lead to Bellamy writing the program that contained the "Pledge of Allegiance."

The Bellamy "Nationalism" movement was so large that in the 1930's Edward Weeks, Charles Beard, and

John Dewey all listed Edward Bellamy's book as being nearly as influential as Karl Marx's "Das Kapital" (1867). Back then, they intended that as a compliment, not as a condemnation.

The book "Edward Bellamy Abroad" by the author Sylvia E. Bowman states that Edward Bellamy's book was translated into every major language including German, Russian and Chinese. Bowman's book is 543 pages long, and details the Bellamy inspiration to socialists worldwide. Bowman's book devotes an entire chapter (55 pages) to describe Edward Bellamy's influence in Germany, including the years leading up to the formation of the National Socialist German Workers' Party (Nazis). Nevertheless, Bowman is another example of an author who failed to make the discoveries made by Dr. Curry and described in this book.

The author Timothy Kubal, in "Cultural Movements and Collective Memory: Christopher Columbus and the Rewriting of the National Origin Myth," states that in 1891 Francis Bellamy promoted socialism in an article entitled "Socialism versus anarchy," published in the Nationalist Club's newspaper, the Arena.

The book "The Pledge of Allegiance" by Dr. John W. Baer states that in the Pledge of Allegiance, Francis Bellamy is expressing the ideas of his first cousin (Edward). Francis was a vice president of the Christian Society of Socialists, affiliated with Edward's Nationalist movement (Francis worked as a lieutenant in the campaign to impose their "military socialism" upon the entire U.S. economy).

The book "Looking Backward" (by Edward Bellamy)

was written in 1888 and described a fantasy about life in the year 2000. It is a totalitarian society where all private transactions are outlawed; where the government places all men in an "industrial army" (a Bellamy phrase) explicitly modeled on the military; where the government has taken over all schools as a government monopoly for the "industrial army" system to achieve "military socialism" (a Bellamy phrase); where everything is nationalized. All in this paragraph was portrayed as a utopia. The Bellamy cousins admired the military, and said it was very efficient, and they wanted the military system to be imposed upon all of society.

- 4 -

FASCIST SALUTES
& THE PLEDGE OF ALLEGIANCE

Francis Bellamy's Pledge of Allegiance was published first in the Youth's Companion Magazine in 1892. That article shows the following: The original pledge began with a military salute for the phrase "I pledge allegiance...." and then the right-arm military salute was extended outward toward the flag for the rest of the pledge so that the right arm was held aloft at an angle directed at the flag, as if to signify, "There is the flag."

The following paragraph is an excerpt showing the pledge as printed for the first time in the 1892 edition of the Youth's Companion Magazine:

At a signal from the Principal the pupils, in ordered ranks, hands to the side, face the Flag. Another signal is given; every pupil gives the Flag the military salute - right hand lifted, palm downward, to a line with the forehead and close to it. Standing thus, all repeat together, slowly: "I pledge allegiance to my Flag and the Republic for which it stands; one Nation, indivisible, with Liberty and Justice for all." At the words, "to my Flag," the right hand is extended gracefully, palm upward, towards the Flag, and remains in this gesture till the end of the affirmation.; whereupon all hands immediately drop to the side. [end of excerpt]

The impact of the military salute as the origin of the Nazi salute is visible in old film footage of children performing the Pledge of Allegiance. Film footage shows conclusively that the military salute was, in practice, extended straight outward to point at the flag (with the palm down).

The original Youth's Companion article along with other research led to more discoveries by Professor Curry:

(1). Due to the way that the pledge used the gestures sequentially, the military salute led to the Nazi salute. The Nazi salute is an extended (outstretched) military salute. Although the original Youth's Companion description directed that the palm be turned upward, that was not the case in practice. Historic photographs and film show that in practice the palm was down because the pledge was performed casually with the initial military salute perfunctorily stretched straight out toward the flag (palm down, because the military salute is palm down in the USA -but it is not palm down in the British army and in some other countries).

(2). The straight-armed salute of the original Pledge of Allegiance was the source of the salute of the National Socialist German Workers' Party (Nazis).

(3). The gesture was neither an ancient Roman salute nor an ancient Olympic salute, and was not ancient in any way.

The above explains why the media, schools, history museums, and other so-called "educational" outlets, will never show film footage (nor photographs) of the early Pledge of Allegiance. They do not want to concede the pledge's putrid past (and its putrid present, and its putrid future).

- 5 -

FLAGS OF FASCISM?

Which is more similar to the swastika flag: the Confederate flag or the U.S. flag? Which is more of a symbol of racism?

The Confederate flag is a popular answer in government schools (socialist schools), with students who are ignorant of the history of the U.S. flag, its Pledge of Allegiance, and the Bellamys.

That answer changes when students learn that the U.S. flag and its Pledge of Allegiance were the origin of the Nazi salute and Nazi behavior (e.g. robotic chanting). It was also the origin of the Nazi salute and Nazi behavior under the swastika flag.

The government (socialist) schools that Bellamy promoted imposed segregation by law and taught racism as official policy. Those racist policies even outlasted German national socialism. Some critics argue that official segregation and racism continues today in the socialist schools, albeit in different forms.

Within the racist schools, segregated classrooms of

black children were forced to perform the Nazi salute and to chant mechanically en masse at the ring of a bell for 12 years of their lives. People who refused were expelled, beaten, imprisoned, and even lynched. It is impossible to quantify the damage that was done and that continues to be done as a result of socialist racism.

Even after some school segregation ended the government continued its racism and used forced busing to destroy black neighborhoods.

The U.S. continues to hold the worst world records for imprisoning blacks and otherwise ruining their lives with felony convictions for victimless crimes and fabricated arrests.

Francis Bellamy and Edward Bellamy admired how the military had killed so many Americans during the War for Southern Independence. It was the source of their Nationalism and their national socialism. The phrase "one nation indivisible" in Bellamy's pledge reveals his perception of the war: not against slavery, but to reverse the South's declaration of independence in order to "preserve the union."

After the War of Northern Aggression, the pledge enabled Christian Socialists to lead a daily witch hunt for disloyalty within government schools (socialist schools) each morning at the ring of a bell.

Bellamy did that despite the history that is celebrated each 4th of July: when slaveholders seceded from their country (Britain) and soon thereafter waved the red, white, and blue flag over their seceded slave-holding rebel land.

Bellamy wanted everyone to chant his Pledge of

Allegiance to the nation and its flag - a flag that had flown over a nation of slavery since the flag's creation so long ago.

Confederacy groups begin their meetings with the Pledge of Allegiance to the U.S. flag.

The U.S. flag resembles the First Confederate national flag (not the Confederate battle flag with the "X" letter shape of the St. Andrew's cross). The first Confederate national flag contained three horizontal stripes of equal height, alternating red and white, with a blue square two-thirds the height of the flag as the canton. Inside the canton are white pointed stars of equal size, arranged in a circle, pointing outward, and representing the seceded states. As secession spread, the flag contained thirteen star representing thirteen seceded states (similar to the thirteen seceded states and stars on the original flag of the United States).

Today, whenever the First Confederate national flag is flown (instead of the Confederate battle flag), students from the government's schools do not know what the flag is. If the First Confederate national flag replaced the Confederate battle flag, years would pass before most students from government schools understood what the flag was and that a substitution of flags had been made.

Southerners in the Confederate States of America (CSA) believed they embodied the ideals of the American Revolution, and the earlier secession in 1776.

Abraham Lincoln's Gettysburg Address said the soldiers sacrificed their lives "to the cause of self-determination - that government of the people, by the people, for the people should not perish from the earth."

H.L. Mencken said: "It is difficult to imagine anything more untrue. The Union soldiers in the battle actually fought against self-determination; it was the Confederates who fought for the right of people to govern themselves."

The Pledge of Allegiance is a slave's pledge of allegiance to his master.

Francis wanted the government to take over all schools as a government monopoly in order to create the "industrial army" system to achieve "military socialism" (a Bellamy phrase). Bellamy touted "military socialism" (the phrase he and his cousin Edward Bellamy used) because they so admired how the military destroyed the South that they wanted the military system imposed on all of society. Francis was spreading the dogma of his comrade Edward, the author of the internationally best-selling socialist book "Looking Backward."

The Bellamys wanted everything to be taken over by government. The pledge of servility put everyone on the road to serfdom. They are one of the origins of modern feudalism, crony socialism and the military-socialism complex. The book "Looking Backward" portrayed their goal as a utopia.

The pledge continues to be a daily witch hunt for disloyalty within government schools (socialist schools) each morning at the ring of a bell.

- 6 -

FREEMASONRY, FASCISM, & FRANCIS

Francis J. Bellamy and James Bailey Upham (the person who assisted Bellamy in creating the Pledge of Allegiance) were both Freemasons. Bellamy was a Mason in Little Falls Lodge No. 181, in Little Falls, NY (and a genuine Masonic Lodge website, the Grand Lodge of British Columbia and Yukon, openly and proudly boasts of his membership in Freemasonry). James Bailey Upham was a Mason in the Converse Lodge in Malden Massachusetts (Also see "Twenty-Three Words" by Margarette S. Miller).

Edward Bellamy's father-in-law was a Baptist minister who'd been forced out of his church for becoming a Freemason.

Freemasonry fit the Bellamy dogma of "military socialism." Regimentation and ritualism appealed to Masons like Francis Bellamy and James Upham. Freemasonry touts an intricate mythology, veiled in allegory, and manifested by pledges, uniforms, symbols, and rituals.

Within the Masonic order, Upham was a Knights Templar, the most esteemed and discriminating order. The word "discriminating" is a double entendre in that the Knights Templar is the only Masonic order that excluded (and still excludes) non-Christians (people they classify as Jews, Muslims and atheists), according to the book "To the Flag" by Richard J. Ellis (another book about the pledge that fails to ask or answer the question of the pledge as the origin of the Nazi salute).

The Order of the Knights Templar, also known as the American Rite, is the highest order in the York Rite, the largest Masonic organization in the United States. According to the book "The Pledge of Allegiance" by Dr. John W. Baer, it is equal to a Thirty-Third Degree Scottish Rite Mason, the top of the Masonic hierarchy.

The Masons also exclude women and there is a separate "auxiliary" organization that accepts women and it is called the "Order of the Eastern Star" and its symbol is a star turned upside down.

Bellamy was a bigot. Bellamy's racism is shown in many examples, including these: "Where every man is a lawmaker, every dull-witted or fanatical immigrant admitted to our citizenship is a bane to the commonwealth," and "Where all classes of society merge insensibly into one another every alien immigrant of inferior race may bring corruption to the stock," and "...there are races which we cannot assimilate without lowering our racial standard, which should be as sacred to us as the sanctity of our homes."

Bellamy wanted the government to take over all schools in order to stamp out individuality and force everyone to be the same (that is what Bellamy and other socialists meant by "equality"). When the government granted his wish, the socialist schools imposed segregation by law and taught racism as official policy.

The 1925 film "The Vanishing American" depicts segregated Native Americans being taught the Nazi salute and Bellamy's robotic chanting in a government school. An infamous photograph that is available on the internet shows African American children performing the Nazi salute and chanting Bellamy's Pledge of Allegiance in their segregated socialist school. Another infamous photograph shows segregated Japanese Americans performing the American Nazi salute in an internment camp during another one of Franklin Delano Roosevelt's many socialist programs or pogroms (the photograph is by Dorothea Lange, a photographer who worked for the ominously titled Resettlement Administration (RA); for the FERA (forerunner of today's FEMA); for the FSA; and under the auspices of the USDA).

During Bellamy's time (and today?), the Knights Templar and Masons in general lamented what they called capitalism's crass commercialism, selfish materialism, and excessive individualism. That view fit nicely with the socialist views of Upham and Bellamy.

Bellamy was hired by Upham's uncle-by-marriage, Daniel S. Ford, to work for the Youth's Companion Magazine, a popular magazine where Upham already worked. Upham and Bellamy collaborated to write the Pledge of Allegiance for the magazine.

Upham and Ford were aware of Francis Bellamy's socialist dogma before Bellamy was hired. Bellamy was involved in so much radicalism and subversion that he was forced out of the ministry of his Boston church for his socialist sermons, including topics like "Jesus the Socialist." Bellamy was a vice president of the Christian Society of Socialists.

Bellamy's dogma was the same argument used later by German Christians under Hitler's socialism and under Germany's hooked cross (see Gerhard Hahn, *Christuskreuz und Hakenkreuz*, Schriftenreihe der "Deutschen Christen" Hannovers, Nr. 1 (1934)). In the German churches, the Christian Cross was next to the Hooked Cross. In American churches, the Christian Cross was (and is) next to the U.S. flag, whose pledge was the origin of the Nazi salute, and whose mechanical chanting continues today.

The Pledge of Allegiance was a small part of a much larger program (authored and/or supervised by Bellamy) in the Youth's Companion magazine. The larger program included a reference to Rome. The program also included hymns, prayer, and various references to the bible and God, including the phrase "under God."

It is hard to believe that some people object to the Pledge of Allegiance only on the grounds of the two-word deification (added in 1954). Some argue falsely that Bellamy would have objected to the phrase and imply that Bellamy was an atheist. People who object only to the two-word deification "under God" are strange and fail to see the forest because they are staring at a single tree.

- 7 -

NAZIS & MASONS

Freemasonry was involved in the formation of the Nazi Party. Rudolf Glandeck von Sebottendorff (born Adam Alfred Rudolph Glauer in 1875) and Hermann Pohl (founder of the fraternity, the German Order Walvater of the Holy Grail). Sebottendorff had been initiated into the Rite of Memphis, a Freemason group. Sebottendorf and Pohl established a fraternity in Munich known as the "Thule Gesellschaft," on August 17, 1918 (see "Anti-masonry Frequently Asked Questions," Section 6, version 2.9, of the Grand Lodge of British Columbia and Yukon). It was originally called the "Studiengruppe für germanisches Altertum" (Study Group for German Antiquity).

On January 5, 1919, the Thule group merged with the Committee of Independent Workers, renaming themselves the Deutsche Arbeiter-Partei (the German Workers' Party). Adolf Hitler claimed he was the seventh member to join this group and he changed its name to the National Socialist German Workers' Party in 1920.

Sebottendorff authored the novel "Der Talisman des Rosenkreuzers" (The "Rosicrucian Talisman," and the "Rosicrucian" combines the words "rose" and "cross").

Another of Sebottendorff's books "Bevor Hitler Kam" ("Before Hitler Came" 1933) was banned in Bavaria. That book stated that Hitler was influenced by the Thule Gesellschaft.

The Thule dogma was influenced by occultists such as Adolf Lanz (aka Lanz von Liebenfels 1874-1954), Guido von List (1848-1919), and Madam Helena Blavatsky (who also used the swastika symbol).

In 1899, Adolf Lanz founded his Order of the New Templars, and the name was inspired by the Knights Templar. In his related magazine "Ostara" he used the swastika symbol as well as the kruckenkreuz (aka croix potent). Lanz' magazine was noticed by Hitler. In 1934, a year after Hitler came to power, Lanz claimed that the Order of the New Templars was the "first manifestation of the [German National Socialist] Movement..."

There are photographs of James Upham that show him wearing the uniform of the Knights Templar. Although Upham, Bellamy, and other Masons criticized crass commercialism and capitalism as part of their socialist ideology, they enjoyed sashes, gloves, belts, swords, plumes, and other rich regalia.

While Upham and the Bellamys promoted "military socialism," the Masonic uniform at that time (as worn by Upham) was modeled after the military and included various medals and badges that were similar to those adopted later by the National Socialist German Workers' Party.

One of the symbols is called a Maltese Cross and others are what the Nazi's called the "Ritterkreuz" (Rider Cross, Knight's Cross or Iron Cross).

It is doubtful that any Mason today would still wear Upham's uniform publicly because those symbols became almost as notorious as the swastika (Hakenkreuz or "hooked cross") under the National Socialist German Workers' Party.

The Freemasons suffer faults that are shared by other civic groups. A review of web sites for most civic groups reveals no understanding of private property rights, supply and demand pricing, laissez-faire economics, free markets, individual rights, and capitalism.

A review of most civic groups reveals vague altruistic clichés that translate into active support for expanding government and various socialist schemes.

Freemasons begin meetings with the Pledge of Allegiance today. They do it because of Francis Bellamy and James Upham, both Freemasons and both socialists, who created the original 1892 chant.

Bellamy and Upham took advantage of the vague socialism of the Freemasons (and similar civic groups) to spread their dogma. It continues to happen even though the original straight-arm salute has been replaced.

In the past, the Masons excluded people that they defined as "negroes, mulattoes or women." The groups in many states would not admit people they classified as "cripples."

While freedom of association is an important right, those types of policies are pernicious when people support government institutions, because government institutions are utilized to impose such policies by force of law. That is what happened in the USA.

In the USA, the Bellamy and Upham dogma supported a government takeover of education in order to have children mimic the military and to produce an "industrial army" (a Bellamy term). The government's schools imposed segregation by law and taught racism as official policy. The USA's behavior was an example for three decades before the Nazis.

American socialism was similar to German socialism at that time because Jehovah's Witnesses, blacks, and the Jewish, and others attended government schools that dictated segregation, taught racism, and punished children who refused to perform the straight-arm salute and mechanical chanting of the Pledge of Allegiance to the flag. There were acts of violence. There were incidents in which government schools attempted to take children away from parents on the grounds of "unfit parenting" if the parents would not force the children to chant the pledge and perform the gesture.

When Jesse Owens competed in the 1936 Olympics in Nazi Germany he performed the initial part of the American gesture to the flag (the military salute part), but did not perform the straight-arm gesture, as he did not want the gesture to be misunderstood as a salute to Adolf Hitler. Other photographs show U.S. athletes performing the American stiff-armed salute (the classic Nazi salute) at the Olympics in 1936 and at earlier Olympic games. The U.S.'s Nazi gesture had been adopted as the Official Olympic salute, and the Olympics had helped to spread the U.S.'s gesture globally.

At that time, many of Owens' fans in the U.S. attended (and had attended) segregated government schools where the pledge was performed with the straight-armed gesture, and where they were required by law to chant it mechanically on command in government schools (socialist schools). The U.S. practice of official racism and segregation in government schools even outlasted the Nazi Party after its defeat in WWII, and into the 1960's and beyond.

In 1936, the military salute alone (as performed by Jesse Owens at the Olympics) was not the customary civilian salute to the U.S. flag. The 1936 Olympics and the war that followed all added to the 1942 interference by Congress regarding the flag ritual at that time. Congress eventually eliminated the military salute, and also eliminated the straight-arm salute. Congress legislated in favor of the hand-over-the-heart. The gesture was not officially altered by Congress until 1942, after the beginning of WWII. That is when the modern hand-over-the-heart was enacted into law.

The Mason's had (and have?) a practice of discriminating against many people to exclude them from their groups, but they did not exclude Germans.

It is important to remember that during all that time, German-American Freemasons attended racist and segregated government schools in the U.S. and saluted with a straight-arm salute toward the U.S. flag, as written by the self-proclaimed national socialists (and Masons) Francis Bellamy and James Bailey Upham. That was a long time before (and leading up to) the adoption of the salute by the National Socialist German Workers' Party.

The National Socialist German Workers' Party was influenced by German-Americans who were already national socialists in the United States. Some German-Americans joined the German American Bund movement (Deutsch-Amerikanischer Volksbund) to support national socialists in Germany before WWII. The bund began as the Friends of New Germany in Chicago in 1933. This group traced its roots to the Teutonia Society and National Socialist Party, both active in the USA during the 1920s.

There was much travel between the U.S. and Germany (the Hindenburg zeppelin disaster occurred in 1937 in New Jersey).

A specific source of Adolf Hitler learning the stiff-armed salute and mechanical chanting from the United States would be Ernst "Putzi" Hanfstaengl, one of Hitler's intimates, who attended schools in the USA.

Another source of the gesture was President Woodrow Wilson during World War I. Socialist leaders in the USA (e.g. Woodrow Wilson) were using the gesture before socialist leaders in Italy and Germany aped them (along with robotic chanting in unison on command in government schools (socialist schools)). President Woodrow Wilson insisted that all school children recite the pledge, and he led them into doing so using the American Nazi salute. After World War II, the Bellamy salute that Wilson so loved became less popular. The robotic chanting on command continued daily (with an altered hand gesture), and it haunts children to this day.

From 1892 through 1942, public officials (including U.S. presidents, congressmen, governors, state legislators and everyone down to the local dog catcher) performed the American Nazi salute and were photographed and filmed doing so. Those photos and films are rare because people don't want to know the truth. Public officials in the USA who preceded the German socialist (Hitler) and the Italian socialist (Mussolini) were sources for the stiff-armed salute (and robotic chanting) in those countries and other foreign countries.

- 8 -

SWASTIKAS & FASCISM

The swastika was a popular symbol in the United States during the time that the Bellamy cousins were promoting their "industrial army" under their "military socialism" in their government schools (socialist schools) with their Pledge of Allegiance.

American soldiers used the swastika as their symbol early in World War I, and up to 1941, against Germany. The symbol was used by Americans in the French Escadrille Lafayette; by the 45th Infantry Division; and on Boeing P-12 planes. The symbol was used by the Krit Motor Car company (based in the U.S.) on vehicles exported to Europe and used in World War I.

An American postcard pre-dating World War II, and circa 1915 (World War I) shows the swastika joined with the U.S.'s flag. The postcard reads "May our glorious flag and this 'lucky star' guide you and keep you wherever you are." The swastika is the 'lucky star' under the U.S.'s flag. At that time, the flag was worshiped with the Nazi salute under threat of prosecution in schools that imposed segregation by law and taught racism as official policy.

Boy Scouts in the USA wore medals bearing the swastika and performed the Nazi salute for the Pledge of Allegiance and adopted (as did Girl Scouts) America's Nazi salute as their own salute. Scouts traveled internationally to spread their paramilitary practices and military socialism.

A Freemasonry group -the Grand Lodge of British Columbia and Yukon- displays on its website a photograph of what it identifies as a Navajo Indian carpet (circa 1925) decorated with the Freemason symbol between two swastikas. That Freemason site also boasts that Francis Bellamy, author of the Pledge of Allegiance, was a Mason. The site neglects to mention anything about the pledge's early Nazi salute and influence.

The swastika was also used by the Theosophical society, an international group that promoted the socialist schemes of Edward Bellamy. The Theosophical Society, and its leader Helena Blavatsky (from Russia), also promoted odd racial theories, including use of the term "Aryan."

In 1917, socialism was imposed in Russia, renamed the Union of Soviet Socialist Republics. The first new paper money (rubles) after the socialist revolution displayed swastikas in the same "S" letter style that later became the symbol of German socialism.

At the turn of 1918-19, and unmentioned in "Mein Kampf," Hitler wore a red brassard and supported the short-lived Bavarian Soviet Republic, according to Thomas Weber in the book "Hitler's First War."

There is something important that is not in Weber's book: Perhaps the Bavarian Soviet Republic experience played a role in the German National Socialist leader (Hitler) adopting a swastika symbol that had been used as a symbol of socialism by Soviet socialists on ruble currency (in 1917 and 1918).

The Bavarian Soviet Republic provides more evidence that Adolf Hitler used the swastika to symbolize crossed "S" letters for "socialism" under his National Socialist German Workers Party.

Hitler collaborated with Soviet socialists again in 1939 when German socialists became allies with the Union of Soviet Socialist Republics in a pact to divide up Europe, invading Poland together, and spreading World War II.

German socialists did not refer to their symbol by its popular modern name, "swastika." They called it a "Hakenkreuz." The term "Hakenkreuz" means "hooked cross." To Germans at that time, the Hakenkreuz symbol was a type of domestic (German) cross, not a foreign Sanskrit "swastika." That is one reason why the German term "Hakenkreuz" (hooked cross) is covered up with the word "swastika" today. The term "swastika" continues to be used to slander a foreign symbol in ongoing efforts to hide what German socialists thought about their symbol: that it was a type of cross and, under Hitler, it was altered for use as alphabetical symbolism for "socialism."

The modern misnomer "swastika" was used (and continues to be used) to cover up German socialism's origin in American Christian Socialism, via Francis Bellamy and his cousin Edward Bellamy.

LIBERAL FASCISM

- 9 -

FASCISM'S WHOLECAUST & HOLOCAUST

The Bellamy dogma was the same dogma that led to the modern Christian Crusades of Christian socialism, and to history's worst bloodbath under the socialist Wholecaust (of which the Holocaust was a part): ~50 million slaughtered under Stalin and Soviet Socialism; ~40 million under Mao and Chinese socialism; ~20 million under German socialism. Under socialism the cross (both the old Christian cross and the hooked-cross of socialism) continued to represent human sacrifice and death. The state is the only modern religion that continues to demand human sacrifices.

The socialist Dark Ages included the modern inquisitions for much of the world: millions were tortured, interrogated and persecuted as "heretics" against socialism. Family members would denounce each other in show trials. It was much worse than the earlier inquisitions and Dark Ages. Socialists promised heaven on earth but provided hell for everyone not part of the ruling class. It continues in some parts of the world, including North Korea.

Today, in the United States, Bellamy's Pledge of Allegiance continues as a daily socialist inquisition in government (socialist) schools. From its origin in 1892, the pledge remains the first bullying that begins each school day for small children up through high school graduation.

In the past, the pledge inspired beatings, arrests, school expulsions, and lynchings. E. V. Starr of Kansas was sentenced in 1918 to twenty years of hard labor for abusive language toward the U.S. flag. A federal judge felt powerless to reverse the lower state court's sentence even though the judge believed that Starr was "more sinned against than sinning." The mob that instigated Starr's persecution, he wrote in his opinion, had descended into the kind of "fanaticism" that fueled the "tortures of the Inquisition."

According to the Bellamy cousins, Jesus was a socialist and Christianity is socialism. Under that dogma, socialism (via the old Crusades) initiated the socialist bloodbath long before it was exceeded in the later socialist Wholecaust (the modern socialist Crusades, of which the Holocaust was a part).

Francis Bellamy's interpretation of Christianity is similar to "Christian atheism" - rejecting belief in the God of Christianity, but embracing the supposed teachings of "Jesus the socialist." In comparison, a person is a Marxist for following Marx's ideas while not thinking Marx was a god. With that logic, the socialists Stalin, Mao, and Hitler would have been "Christians," if they believed that Christ was a socialist who wanted everyone to spread socialism. Every monster believes that, if there are gods, then the gods support him.

The Bellamy cousins believed that they promoted Our Lord and Savior "socialist government" as foretold by Jesus the socialist. Through Christian socialism, Bellamy touted an omnipotent/omniscient entity (government or God) ruling over everyone. Many people believe in a supreme power who rules beneficently over all of humanity. That is the essence of both socialism and religion. The question must be asked: How do you separate church and state when the state is your church?

Socialists are faith-healers fleecing the gullible crowds. Miracles are promised for the worship of gov via the pledge: magically "free gifts" from gov (healthcare, schools, sports stadia, and more); fiat paper money printed at will; endless socialist debt to pay for it all. It is the revelation of Edward Bellamy's utopia.

Christianity and religion are often maligned for the number of deaths they caused. Socialists are often maligned for the number of deaths they caused. Whatever those numbers are, they are combined into one number under the Bellamy dogma. According to Bellamy, Christianity was socialism. Jesus was a socialist touting the same dogma as Stalin, Mao and Hitler. The millions killed by Stalin, Mao and Hitler were caused by the same dogma touted by Jesus and Christianity: Socialism.

Under the Bellamy dogma, Christ was to a large degree a non-religious figure whose true message was socialism. Bellamy's concept of Christianity (Christian socialism) is not inconsistent with the atheism of Stalin and Mao. Socialism is the actual message and goal,

Christ was simply a messenger of socialism, similar to his modern angels in the socialists Stalin, Mao, and Hitler.

Modern Socialist Crusades had many other similarities to the old Christian Crusades, because the modern crusades had: aggressive expansion attempts by modern socialists; all "sins" (all atrocities) are justified and forgiven to whosoever took up the cause of socialism. The crusades reinforced the connection between socialism and militarism. Similar to the old Crusades, the modern socialist Crusades were military campaigns, consistent with the Bellamy dogma of "military socialism" and similar socialistic militarism under Stalin, Mao and Hitler. The modern socialist crusaders often pillaged the countries through which they invaded in the typical medieval manner. Socialists often retained much of the territory gained rather than returning it (e.g. the territories desired and acquired by the Union of Soviet Socialist Republics under the pact between German socialism and Soviet socialism).

The unmatched bloodbath of socialism inspired two new fields of study: anarchaeology and misanthropology. Anarchaeology is the study of how people throughout history have progressed and thrived with limited government (minarchy) or with no government at all. Misanthropology is the study of how governments cause chaos, and create poverty, misery and mass slaughter that destroys civilizations. Both fields consist of members (Anarchaeologists and misanthropologists) who often study the worst examples in history: the socialist Wholecaust (of which the Holocaust was a part).

Modern Holocaust museums will triple in size when they include the entire socialist Wholecaust.

There are many ways that the Bellamy dogma spread globally including the World's Fair from May 1893 to October 30, 1893. The German firm Krupp had a pavilion of artillery at the Fair, which cost approximately one million dollars.

Another example of how the dogma spread appears in an obituary for Edward Bellamy: "It is stated that Emperor William purchased 1,000 copies of 'Looking Backward,' which he distributed among the students and working classes of Germany." (obituary dateline Springfield, Mass., May 22, 1898, "The Author of 'Looking Backward' has Passed Away").

In January 1892, in preparation for the World's Columbian Fair, the Youth's Companion assigned Francis Bellamy to be manager for the National Public School Celebration of Columbus Day on October 11, 1892. In 1492, Native Americans discovered Columbus lost at sea. Columbus Day commemorates the explorer Christopher Columbus in a country named after Amerigo Vespucci, who exposed Columbus' mistaken belief that Columbus had visited Asia or India. The country had been previously "discovered" by Leif Erikson and plenty of others, including the aborigines (the 1925 film "The Vanishing American" shows Native Americans being taught the Nazi salute and Bellamy's robotic chanting in a government school).

The Columbus Day holiday inspired Bellamy to write his "Address for Columbus Day" entitled "The Meaning of the Four Centuries," which was part of the program that included the Pledge of Allegiance.

Francis Bellamy's work (including his Columbus Day program in which the Pledge of Allegiance was a small part) contained hymns, prayers, the phrase "under God," Bible references, and more to tie socialism to the cross and Christianity. It was socialism as a religion.

Bellamy's plan to spread his dogma globally was boosted when Bellamy became chairman of a committee to form a World Congress of Youth at the Columbia Exposition in Chicago in 1893. The World's Youth Congress Auxiliary (or World Congress Auxiliary) asked The Youth's Companion magazine (where Francis Bellamy worked) to organize the scheme. A. F. Nightingale was president of the Youth's World Congress. More details are provided in a newspaper article, "Youths at the World's Fair," from the Daily Gleaner on August 22, 1892 ("The Gleaner" continues to publish in Jamaica and states that it was established in 1834). The article explains that the congress would be composed of youths of all nations of the World (and many countries are listed including Germany, Russia, Italy, France and "countries of the Orient"). The youths will "stand before the generation to follow us as witnesses of the humanizing power of the World's Exposition of 1893, and be inspired by its influence to higher and more useful careers, making the fulfillment of its great promises their noblest claim to history." The "humanizing power" that Bellamy brought to the World's Exposition of 1893 (and the fulfillment of Bellamy's "noblest" claim to history) was the Nazi salute and robotic chanting to flags daily in military formation in government schools (socialist schools).

The "Brotherhood of man" cliché that is used in the newspaper article was a popular cliché with the international Theosophical Society, which promoted the dogma of Francis Bellamy and Edward Bellamy. The Theosophical Society also utilized the swastika symbol to promote its socialist dogma.

Bellamy's international aspiration for his World Youth Congress is one of the reasons why Bellamy's original pledge did not reference the "flag of the United States of America." Bellamy wrote his pledge so that it could be adopted by other countries. He wanted to spread military socialism worldwide.

Did those "coming leaders of mankind" from the World Youth Congress include people who became supporters of the socialists Stalin, Mao, and Hitler?

- 10 -

NAZISM & AMERICAN FASCISM

"Nazis" did NOT call themselves "Nazis." The modern misnomer "Nazi" was used (and continues to be used) to cover up German socialism's origin in American Christian Socialism, via Francis Bellamy and his cousin Edward Bellamy.

"Nazis" did NOT call themselves "Fascists" (also see author Jonah Goldberg's "Liberal Fascism: The Secret History of the American Left, From Mussolini to the Politics of Meaning" citing the work of the historian Dr. Rex Curry). The term "Fascist" is also used to hide the fact that Mussolini was a long-time socialist leader and socialist journalist, that he acquired the name "Il Duce" ("the leader") as a socialist, and that he learned America's stiff-armed salute as a socialist leader.

In Hitler's "Mein Kampf" (1925), and in Leni Riefenstahl's film "Triumph of the Will" (1934), the word "socialist" is used throughout and the words "Nazi" and "Fascist" are never used -not a single time- in reference to the National Socialist German Workers'

Party.

"Triumph of the Will" shows the National Socialist German Workers' Party parading its industrial army of military socialism. In keeping with their socialist dogma, Hitler is praised as an "epitome of altruism" and the speakers refer to each other as "comrades" who will cause a "revolution of the people and workers" to end "class struggle" and create "egalitarianism."

The double "S" letters and sounds of the word "swastika" and "socialism" were (and are) interchangeable. They are, in a sense, mutually onomatopoeic. They are linked in a way that the four letter N-word (Nazi) is not. In Hitler's stylized symbol, the swastika is synonymous with, and is a mnemonic reminder of, his socialism.

Hitler's "S" shape for the swastika added to the ignorant belief that German socialists called their symbol a swastika, in that the word "swastika" starts with the letter "S" and has two "S" sounds (and letters) in its spelling, as does the word "socialism."

Although the swastika was an ancient symbol for "good luck" in India (and the word "swastika" is Sanskrit), that is not why it was used by German socialists.

If Hitler was aware of a general meaning of "good luck" for the symbol, then that would have encouraged him in his use of the symbol for his socialist dogma. All socialists mistakenly believe that their policies are "auspicious good luck" for everyone.

There is a question whether Hitler even knew of the term "swastika" or that the symbol was an ancient good-luck symbol in India. Additional support comes from John Toland's lengthy book "Adolf Hitler: The Definitive Biography." Toland asserts (page 86) that when the leader of the National Socialist German Workers' Party adopted the symbol, it was already in use as a symbol for another socialist group, a fact known by Hitler when selecting the symbol. Toland writes "Drexler [Anton Drexler] suggested calling their group the German Socialist Party (the same name of a similarly motivated party founded a year earlier [1916?] in Bohemia [Czechoslovakia], whose emblem incidentally, was the swastika)."

Based on Toland's book and other sources, there is a question whether the leader of the National Socialist German Workers' Party was even aware of any meaning for the symbol other than as a symbol of an existing socialist group.

Another entry in Toland's book (page 183) references the use of the hooked cross under Hans Knirsch, founder of the National Socialist Workers Party in Czechoslovakia, a group that was also known as the Sudetendeutsche National Sozialistische Partei (Sudeten-German National Socialist Party).

If the swastika was a symbol of the Sudetendeutsche National Sozialistische Partei, then that use provides additional evidence of alphabetical symbolism for the swastika's two overlapping "S" letters: "Sudeten Socialism" or even "Southern Socialism." The word "Sudeten" came to mean "Southern" for many Germans, although the original etymology is unclear.

Toland also notes that the swastika was long a symbol

of the Teutonic Knights and had been used by Lanz Von Liebenfels, the Thule Society and a number of other groups before Hitler's Socialist Party.

Another example of the swastika's use is at the Abbey Lambach where Hitler attended as a youth. Revealing differences exist between the swastika symbols of Abbey Lambach, of the Thule Society, and in the symbol used later by German socialists. If the two earlier symbols influenced the later Nazi symbol, then they prove Hitler's alteration of the symbols to more closely reflect overlapping "S" letters in the later Nazi symbol.

The book "Swastika: the earliest known symbol and its migrations" (1894) by Thomas Wilson shows that the symbol was used in and around ancient Germany and worldwide. The following is from Wilson's book (page 771):

"Dr. Schliemann found many specimens of Swastika in his excavations at the site of ancient Troy on the hill of Hissarlik. They were mostly on spindle whorls, and will be described in due course. He appealed to Professor Max Muller for an explanation, who, in reply, wrote an elaborate description, which Dr. Schliemann published in the book 'Ilios.'

Professor Muller commences with a protest against the word "Swastika" being applied generally to the symbol, because it may prejudice the reader or the public in favor of its Indian origin. Muller says:

*'I do not like the use of the word svastika outside of India. It is a word of Indian origin and has its history and definite meaning in India. * * * The occurrence of*

such crosses in different parts of the world may or may not point to a common origin, but if they are once called Svastika the vulgus profanum will at once jump to the conclusion that they all come from India, and it will take some time to weed out such prejudice.'"

Muller's prediction was amazing in its accuracy: The word "swastika" was used enough that it became the prevailing term, even as a substitute for the actual German word "Hakenkreuz" and many people concluded falsely that all such symbols, including Hitler's Hakenkreuz, were references to India's swastika.

Hitler's Hakenkreuz was not always called a "swastika" outside of Germany. In the U.S., in the UK, and elsewhere, it was also called "hakenkreuz" or "hooked cross" or "crooked cross" or "armed cross."

Today, the term "swastika" is used to slander a foreign symbol in an ongoing effort to cover-up what German socialists thought about their symbol. The media are as unwilling to report the facts about the swastika as they are unwilling to print a historic photograph of the Pledge of Allegiance's early Nazi gesture.

Before German socialism, the swastika symbol was usually oriented horizontally (as if it was drawn within a square) and was pointed left or right (see Wilson's book and illustrations therein).

During Hitler's early life, Hitler viewed the symbol pointed left or right and oriented horizontally (as if it was drawn within a square). A drawing by Hitler (he had been an aspiring artist) shows a fireplace mantel decorated with two of the symbols, both horizontal; one points left and the other points right. That use changed during the existence of the German Socialist Party. Hitler presided over the symbol's mutation. Under Hitler, the swastika became a socialist cipher, and a doppelsieg for a doppelgänger.

Hitler's modification turned the Nazi symbol 45 degrees to the horizontal (as if it was drawn within a diamond shape). The change also turned the Nazi symbol to point the arms rightward in newer, future uses. That also became the official version displayed on the flag. Both transformations to the German socialist symbol emphasized "S" shapes in the orientation.

According to Steven Heller, author of "The Swastika: Symbol Beyond Redemption?" and art director of The New York Times Book Review "Hitler's major contribution was to reverse the direction of the swastika."

But Hitler did more than merely reverse the direction. That is one of the many discoveries that Heller failed to make, including: (1) the symbol represented "S" letters for "socialism" under Hitler, and (2) the relationship of Hitler's hooked cross and his dogma to Christian socialism, to Francis Bellamy, and to the American Nazi salute from the Pledge of Allegiance.

- 11 -

ADOLF HITLER: MAN OF SOCIALISM

Hitler changed the Hakenkreuz, and Hitler changed his own signature in a similar way. Rarely seen autographs from Hitler show that he evolved his signature "Adolf Hitler" into "S Hitler." It was a declaration of his socialism every time he signed his name: as if he was signing "Socialist Hitler."

Most people have never seen Hitler's signature. That is because the media never display Hitler's signature and do not want readers to know what it reveals.

Ernst "Putzi" Hanfstaengl (an intimate of Hitler's), also signed his name with a similar "swastika" flourish. Hanfstaengl, educated in the U.S., might have encouraged Hitler to adopt the American Nazi salute, as well as the "swastika" style signature.

There are signatures from other Hitler underlings that appear to use a "swastika" style flourish.

German military medals were cast with raised lettering that displays Hitler's "S" style signature.

In 1920, Hitler decided that the National Socialist

German Workers' Party needed its own insignia. The new flag had to be "a symbol of our own struggle" as well as "highly effective as a poster." (Mein Kampf, Chapter 7 of the 2nd volume, sometimes pg. 495).

In Mein Kampf, Hitler described the new flag: "In red we see the social idea of the movement, in white the nationalistic idea, in the swastika the mission of the struggle for the victory of the Aryan man, and, by the same token, the victory of the idea of creative work..." (pg. 496-497).

In German the quoted reference was: "im Hakenkreuz die Mission des Kampfes fÜr den Sieg des arischen Menschen und zugleich mit ihm auch den Sieg des Gedankens der schaffenden Arbeit,"

In his own words, Hitler used the word "sieg" twice and can be interpreted as stating that the swastika is a "sieg" symbol. Also known as "sig runes," the "lightning-bolt" symbols are letters of an ancient Germanic alphabet. An internet image search for "double sig rune," "sig rune," "sieg rune," "sigel rune," or "sowilo" provides more examples. The "sieg" rune corresponds with the letter "S" and was used for "S" in other symbolism.

Hitler's quote has overlapping use of the word "sieg." The word "sieg" means "victory." His symbol represented two "S" letters for "socialism" or "socialism and sieg" (socialism and victory) and is related to "Sieg Heil!" (Hail to Victory) in the sense of "Hail to the Victory of Socialism!" (Hail to the Victory of the National Socialist German Workers' Party).

Hitler's quote refers to the red color and the "social idea of the movement" that ties into socialism for which

Hitler claimed the National Socialist German Workers' Party was struggling for victory.

It began in 1919, when Adolf Hitler joined the German Workers' Party, a socialist group. The group sought a new name that would attract socialists in other groups. Other German socialist groups used terms like "National" and "Socialist" in their titles, and the German Workers' Party adopted "National Socialist German Workers' Party."

Hitler gave the Hakenkreuz symbol the same meaning as the group's new name. For Hitler, the joined "S" letters symbolized socialists joining together as the National Socialist German Workers' Party. The intertwined letter "S" shapes represent "Socialists" unified, or "Socialist Solidarity" and the victory of the National Socialist German Workers' Party bringing socialists together in one large group.

Hitler also wrote: "Two years later, when our squad of hall guards had long since grown into storm detachments, it seemed necessary to give this defensive organization of a young Weltanschhauung a particular symbol of victory, namely a Standard." In German it was: "Zwei Jahre spÄter, als aus der Ordnertruppe schon lÄngst eine viel tausend Mann umfassende Sturmabteilung geworden war, schien es nÖtig, dieser Wehrorganisation der jungen Weltanschauung noch ein besonderes Symbol des Sieges zu geben: die Standarte." Hitler again used the phrase "Symbol des Sieges." In the only comments on the symbol by Hitler, the Sturmabteilung was specifically referenced.

The Sturmabteilung had well-known Nazi banners

that included Hitler's Hakenkreuz-swastika in the old style (horizontal / square), the new style (slanted / diamond), and another banner also utilizing another stylized "S" symbol, for the "SA" (Sturm Abteilung).

The term "Nazi" was (and is) a term of derision used by people against the National Socialists German Workers' Party. Party members did not use the term "Nazi" to refer to themselves. Party members used the terms "socialist" or "national socialist" or the full name of the party.

In the notorious 1934 film "Triumph of the Will" by Leni Riefenstahl, and in the 1925 book "Mein Kampf" by Adolf Hitler, the word "socialist" is used throughout and the words "Nazi" and "Fascist" are never used -not a single time- in reference to the National Socialist German Workers' Party. In the film, they refer to each other as "Kamerads" (comrades).

Stylized "S" letters were used in other symbolism under German National Socialists including Hitler's "SS" Division which used two similarly stylized "S" letters side-by-side for "Schutzstaffel," as compared with the overlapping "S" shapes of the Hakenkreuz / swastika;

Alphabetic lettering in a stylized form is shown in other Nazi-Sozi paraphernalia, in Nazi posters, in German medals, flags, banners, and including but not limited to the symbols of the "NSV" (National Socialist Volkswohlfahrt), and the "T-O" logo of the Todt Organization; and the Technische Nothilfe (abbreviated as TN, TeNo, TENO; literally: Technical Emergency Help).

Swastika-style symbolism is visible today and every

day on the streets as the VW logo. The logo is two identical "V" letters crossed to form the letters "V" and "W" (or a "V" and a "W" letter joined) in a similar "hooked cross" alphabetical style for "Volkswagen." The VW was Hitler's socialist "People's Car" scam that he never produced for "the people" (because he was busy killing them in war).

Franz Xaver Reimspiess, Nikolai Borg, and others have claimed credit for the VW logo. Borg, a young commercial artist impressed others when he won the competition for the creation of a logo for the "Deutsche Jugendherbergswerk." Borg said that he was invited to draw the Volkswagen car logo in a request from high-up: Dr. Ing. Fritz Todt, with the "Organization Todt" the general inspector for roads and a militarily organized building troop used in the entire theater of war (boasting its own alphabetical symbol in the conjoined letters "O" and "T" for its logo). Borg stated that he made nine drafts with different connections of the crossed "V" letters, to represent the letters "V" and "W" before his final version emerged. Borg has exhibited photographs in which Borg's VW emblem design was placed on top of the swastika symbol that inspired it, and was created simply by replacing the two crossed "S" letters of the swastika with the two crossed "V" letters (that also form the letters V and W).

Before the VW emblem was created, the symbol for Volkswagen was a swastika encircled by a cogwheel. It was the symbol for the organization that controlled Volkswagen, the socialist trade union organization Deutsche Arbeitsfront (DAF or German Labor Front).

The swastika of the Deutsche Arbeitsfront emblem was the origin of the Volkswagen logo, both philosophically and stylistically.

Similar stylized symbolism is visible in the emblem of the Maybach-Motorenbau; the Trabant Sachsenring automobile. The Automobil Werke Zwickau.

A 1935 Youth's booklet from the National Socialist German Workers' Party shows that youngsters were taught about the "S" shapes of German socialist symbols. The entire 35-page book was uncovered by the symbologist Dr. Curry and it is the only example known to exist. Although the book is in its original German language, the illustrations supplement the text's explanation that common symbols under the National Socialist German Workers' Party often used the "S" shape, including the side-by-side use in the "SS" Division (for "Schutzstaffel") and the overlapping use in the Swastika.

This is a translation of excerpted text in the 1935 Nazi youth's book:

"Today, we are proud of our Germanic heritage; we wish German custom to again be in the lead over everything foreign, and to demonstrate this, the Hitler Youth has taken the old victory sign, the Siegrune, for their flags and armbands.

From the Siegrune "S" one can easily create an "S" "S" form [illustrations showed a stylized rune "S" next to an English-style alphabetic "S" letter]. And the Leader's Schutz-Staffel, which we abbreviate "SS", carries the double-rune "SS" [an illustration showed the classic stylized rune "SS"] as their badge. This victory and salvation rune may also be found in a stretched version, which looks like this [an illustration showed a longer version oriented horizontally]. Many bear a small line in the middle, [an illustration showed the previous version oriented horizontally and a short notch added in the middle] and is then known as Wolfsangel.

"I know something, I know something," Harmut suddenly explained, taking the pencil from his father's hand. "If you superimpose two Wolfsangels, you get a hooked-cross. This is also two Siegrunes." [an illustration showed a Hakenkreuz (swastika)]

"You have made a nice and meaningful discovery, my son," father happily noted, "because the....." [End of quote from that page of the 1935 Nazi youth book].

Each summer thousands of Hitler Youth marched from their hometowns down German roads to meet en masse at Nuremberg to join in the yearly rally and congress of the Nazi-socialists. The notorious film "Triumph of the Will" by Leni Riefenstahl from 1935 was propaganda for the sixth annual rally. The word "socialism" is used in a positive manner throughout the film by the speakers to extol their dogma. The words "Nazi" and "fascist" are never used in the film.

The following words were emphasized as shown in the book "Look to Germany" by Stanley McClatchie:

"NATIONAL SOCIALISM? What does it mean? The true significance of this name given to the German

movement is usually overlooked, and the hasty reader at the breakfast table is prone to see - "National...ism".

THE GERMAN FLAG? What does it look like? The majority of foreigners know that it contains a swastika and believe that this signifies only - "National...ism".

THE FLAG BEARERS? Who are they? The world regards their disciplined ranks, the brown uniforms and reflects - "National...ism".

It is time, however, to wake up!

S O C I A L I S M is the principle word in the title of the Movement. The basic colour in its banner is R E D and those who wear the brown uniforms are C O M R A D E S!"

- 12 -

MUSSOLINI: THE FATHER OF FASCISM

Benito Mussolini was a well-known and long-time socialist leader. Mussolini acquired his title "il duce" - leader- when he was known only as a socialist. As a socialist leader, he began to mimic American socialists in their use of the stiff-armed salute, robotic chanting to flags, the glorification of ancient Rome (or myths about Rome), and the use of the fasces symbol as an emblem of government and socialism.

In ancient Rome, the fasces [fas-eez] was a bundle of sticks bound together. It symbolized "union," or people banded together. Thus, the word "fascist" is related to the word "fagot" (or faggot (British)) as a bundle of wood (see the work of the etymologist Dr. Curry) and via the similar early pronunciation of the words "fasces" and "faggot" (the original Latin term "fasces" was pronounced with a hard letter "C" sound or /k/, not the modern soft letter "C" sound or /s/).

In another bizarre parallel to "Christian Socialism," the phrase "fire and faggot" described punishment of a heretic by burning. Heretics who recanted were forced to display the symbol of a faggot on their shirt sleeve for public humiliation.

Homosexuality was illegal under the old crusades, under early "Christian socialism," and under under the modern socialist crusades of the socialists Stalin, Mao, Hitler, Mussolini, Castro, Pol Pot, et cetera.

The derogatory term for a "male homosexual," 1914, is probably from the earlier use for an old heretical woman, and a reference to the "flaming faggots" (homosexuals were also burned at the stake).

"Heretics" under modern socialist Crusades might include Fanya Kaplan and Charlotte Corday.

The word "fasces" is also related to these words: fascine, fascia, fascinate, fasciatus fish, plantar fasciitis, and many more.

Fascism meant "unionism" to the socialist Benito Mussolini. Mussolini's socialist "unionism" mimicked "soviets" (councils) under Russian socialism (the Union of Soviet Socialist Republics). It was Mussolini's version of socialist syndicalism. Both the Italian and Soviet systems were similar to the organization that arose later under German socialism (the National Socialist German Workers Party).

On December 11, 1914, Mussolini started a political group: Fasci d'azione Rivoluzionaria (Union of Revolutionary Action). It combined two other movements: (1) Fasci d'azione Rivoluzionaria Internazionalista and (2) Fasci Autonomi d'azione Rivoluzionaria (a previous group he started).

"Fasci" referred to Mussolini's socialist union for

socialist revolution. It is similar to the word "faction" in that Mussolini's group was another of many socialist-inspired unions.

The term "fascio" was the Italian word for workers' groups, peasant organizations, labor unions and the other socialist groups where Mussolini had developed a large following.

The Fasci d'azione Rivoluzionaria asserted that it supported socialism, using the famous quote by French socialist Louis Auguste Blanqui, "He who has iron has bread" on the title page of its socialist newspaper, Il Popolo d'Italia. The newspaper announced under its title that it was the "Socialist Daily" (Quotidiano Socialista).

After some indecision, Mussolini supported World War I by appealing to the need for socialists to overthrow the Hohenzollern and Habsburg monarchies in Germany and Austria-Hungary. Mussolini claimed that they had consistently repressed socialism. Mussolini argued that hundreds of thousands of Italians were under Habsburg rule. He asserted that the defeat of Hohenzollern and Habsburg monarchies would help the working class.

Mussolini explained that the war would bring Tsarist Russia to social revolution. He gleefully predicted and supported the socialist revolution that formed the Union of Soviet Socialist Republics (USSR).

In 1919, Mussolini created a new socialist sub-group called "Fasci di combattimento" (also known as the "Fascio nazionale di combattimento"). It referred to his socialist band of combat. It was another use of the word that is similar to "faction" to designate socialist-inspired unions. Socialism is always faction against faction. On 9

November 1921, Mussolini transformed the Fasci Italiani di Combattimento into the National Fascist Party.

Socialism then grew in Germany with the German Workers' Party (Deutsche Arbeiterpartei, DAP) and Hitler's membership therein. On February 24, 1920, Hitler decided to change the name of his group (the DAP). On that date, Mussolini continued to be known as a socialist leader in Italy (although he used the term "fasci" for some of his socialist union sub-groups), and Lenin continued to be known as a socialist leader in the Union of Soviet Socialist Republics. The DAP changed its name to the Nationalsozialistische Deutsche Arbeiterpartei (National Socialist German Workers Party). Hitler did not adopt Mussolini's use of the term "fasci" in any form. Hitler's socialists never self-identified as "Fascists," nor as "Nazis."

Benito Mussolini did NOT say: "Fascism should more appropriately be called Corporatism because it is a merger of State and corporate power." That fake quote was commonly attributed to Mussolini until the attribution was debunked by the veteran historian Dr. Rex Curry.

Some people point to Giovanni Gentile (in "La Dottrina del Fascismo") as the person who created the fake quote that was attributed to Mussolini. "La Dottrina del Fascismo" was written by Giovanni Gentile, and published under Mussolini's name in the Encyclopedia Italiana. However, the only reference to "corporatism" within Genile's article is in section VIII, and NOT in the words of the quote.

There is no original source in Italian that refers to the

quotation. Instead, there is one source in Italian, that translates an American source.

Mussolini never uttered the quote that is attributed to him, and anyone who understands what Mussolini DID say would know that the quote does not describe Mussolini's beliefs.

On July 2, 1926, Mussolini established the Ministry of Corporations and soon thereafter the National Council of Corporations. The wacky Italian socialists also created the Istituto per la Ricostruzione Industriale (IRI). They were ominous parallels to Lenin's Soviet socialism at that time, and what would happen later under Hitler's German socialism, and Roosevelt's American socialism.

Mussolini's Ministry of Corporations organized the Italian economy into 22 "sectoral corporations" (see the Address to the National Corporative Council on November 14, 1933, and the Senate Speech on the Bill Establishing the Corporations on January 13, 1934). The 22 sectoral corporations were the method via which the socialist Mussolini organized his Unionism (Fascism), and his beloved worker's unions, and the economy. It was not until February 5, 1934, that the 22 "corporations" were defined:

1. Social Care & Credit
2. Internal Communications
3. Sea & Air
4. Entertainment
5. Hostelries
6. Professions & Arts
7. Building Construction

8. Water, Gas & Electricity
9. Mining Industries
10. Glass & Ceramics
11. Grains
12. Vegetable, Flower & Fruit Cultivation
13. Wine and Oil Cultivation
14. Livestock & Fish
15. Wood
16. Textiles
17. Clothing
18. Metalworking
19. Machinery
20. Chemicals
21. Liquid Combustibles & Fossil Fuels
22. Paper & Publishing

They were not capitalist "corporations" as is claimed by some socialists in the USA. Socialists deliberately lie about what the socialist Mussolini was saying. Socialists misuse Mussolini's term. Mussolini's "corporations" defeated free markets, businesses, industry, and capitalism.

Mussolini didn't mean the power of big corporations. He meant the power of a large number of individuals working collectively as a bureaucracy or union. That is what he meant by "corporativismo."

Mussolini's term is closer to the concept of a municipal corporation, which is a form of socialism: a government entity that imposes a socialist monopoly on the provision of goods and services.

Socialists say they want to end "corporations" until

they are asked, "You want to end municipal corporations?" After socialists research the meaning of "municipal corporation" they admit that they support the worst form of corporations (municipal corporations), and they share so much with the socialist Mussolini.

Mussolini's doppelganger in the United States was Franklin Delano Roosevelt (FDR). The twin-brothers suckled like wolves on the public teat, competed to be degenerate statists, raced to create new bureaucracies, and spread the roaming mythology of socialism. FDR grew up doing the stiff-armed socialist salute (during the Pledge of Allegiance and also outside of the pledge) long before the socialist leader Mussolini learned it. FDR was merely one in a long line of presidents and other famous Americans who helped teach the notorious gesture to Italy and the world.

Each one of Mussolini's socialist bureaucracies has one or more extant twins among the thousands of alphabet agencies in the United States (and many predate and influenced Mussolini's socialism) including: the Department of Agriculture (USDA 1862); Department of Commerce (1903, 1913); Department of Labor (1903, 1913); Department of the Interior (1849); Social Security Administration; Federal Communications Commission; Department of Health and Human Services; United States Postal Service; Bureau of Land Management; Department of Transportation; Federal Trade Commission; Federal Aviation Administration.

- 13 -

AUGUST LANDMESSER
& OTHER FASCIST VICTIMS

August Landmesser is best known for his appearance in a photograph wherein he refused to perform the stiff-armed salute under German socialism during the launch of a naval training vessel (the Horst Wessel) on 13 June 1936.

No article about Landmesser points out that the same gesture (and persecution of anyone who refused the gesture) was happening in the United States at the same time that it was happening in Germany to Landmesser and others; that the Pledge of Allegiance to the U.S. flag was the origin of the gesture that Landmesser defied. Only in the comments section do people reference the work of Dr. Curry showing that the U.S. was the origin of the Nazi salute and Nazi behavior from the American socialist Francis Bellamy.

No article about Landmesser points out that the same behavior continues in the USA, where only the gesture has changed. Everyday in government schools (socialist schools) children robotically chant in unison on command. The gesture changed to hide the pledge' putrid past. Children are kept ignorant of the history of the quotidian ritual that they are led to perform.

No article about Landmesser explains that a growing wave of students refuse to be bullied into the brainwashing, and are learning the truth about the Pledge's putrid past. No one celebrates their bravery. Such students attract criticism in the media, and even dead silence from people who praise August Landmesser and who have nothing to say about the fact that Americans were persecuted (at the same time that Landmesser was persecuted in Germany) for refusing to perform the nazi salute in the Pledge of Allegiance in the USA.

No article about Landmesser includes photos of Americans circa 1936 that are very similar to the Landmesser photo. Has anyone in the media printed such a photo, or do any of them even have that knowledge?

There are court cases involving prison for Americans who refused to do the Nazi salute for the USA's pledge or who otherwise showed "disrespect" to the U.S. flag. Americans were beaten, imprisoned, even lynched.

The government and government schools deserve blame for that photo of Landmesser. Francis Bellamy deserves blame for Landmesser's predicament.

The photo of Landmesser is powerful and would be more powerful if Americans were not so ignorant of the history of the Pledge of Allegiance as the origin of the Nazi salute and Nazi behavior.

- 14 -

SCHOOLS & PLEDGES:
WE'RE ALL FASCISTS NOW

Francis Julius Bellamy died on August 28, 1931 in Tampa, Florida. Tampa was also the city where Bellamy's Pledge of Allegiance died. A plaque memorializes him and his pledge at the house where he resided on 2926 Wallcraft Avenue.

Although he died in Tampa, Bellamy's remains were moved to Rome, New York, the origin of the "ancient Roman salute" myth that developed from his pledge.

He lived long enough to see the government schools (socialist schools) that he wanted to impose on everyone. He lived long enough to see those schools impose segregation by law and teach racism as official policy, and force children to perform the Nazi salute and robotic chanting daily for 12 years of their lives, upon threat of violence or punishment. He lived through a time when people were beaten, arrested, jailed, imprisoned, and even lynched for defying his pledge.

No evidence has been found that any of the above

bothered him, nor that he considered any of the above to be inconsistent with his dogma of "Christian socialism" and "Military socialism."

His work continues to haunt the world. The American Nazi salute continues to be used in many places, including Mexico, China (including Taiwan), and Russia.

Another subtitle for this book could be "To see or not see Nazi reality." The real "not sees" are people who do not see the socialist symbolism of the swastika and the Pledge of Allegiance. This book was written to educate modern "not-sees."

The cult of socialism was the same as the occult nightmares whispered about Nazism. The swastika was a symbol of "socialist" identity. The chosen people of the National Socialist German Workers' Party were a bizarre para-military fraternity that wanted to evolve and impose a new world order, creating a utopian future, similar to the Military Socialism and Christian Socialism of American socialists (including Francis Bellamy and Edward Bellamy).

Why does socialism inspire misanthropy, atrocities and mass slaughter?

People who adopted the "Double S" and its dogma of socialism preached the sacrifice of everyone. They called it a brave new world, but it was a grave new world.

The misanthropes, necrophiliacs and cannibals caused millions of deaths in the socialist Wholecaust (of which the Holocaust was a part): ~50 million under the Union of Soviet Socialist Republics?; ~40 million under the Peoples' Republic of China?; ~20 million under the National Socialist German Workers' Party? Those eras are known as the modern socialist inquisitions, the modern socialist dark ages (and their inhumanity and death tolls exceeded that of the previous dark ages and of all prior inquisitions). It was the worst death toll in human history and so large that all Holocaust Museums could quadruple in size and scope by adding Wholecaust Museums to document the entire socialist slaughter.

Socialists fancied themselves as the "illuminati," but they were the "deluminati." Today, on world maps, they are the countries where the least light shines at night. Their psycho-pathology set and holds the worst records for extinguishing the life lights of so many.

The socialist psychopathy of the Bellamys continues in the USA today. Many Bellamy policies caused the oppressive domestic government. The pledge continues along with laws mandating that teachers lead the robotic chanting every day for twelve years in the life of each child.

The anti-libertarian government continues to own and operate schools, including the same schools that imposed segregation by law and taught racism as official government policy. The USA's practice of imposing segregation by law (in government schools) and teaching racism as official policy even outlasted the National Socialist German Workers Party into the 1960's and beyond.

After segregation in government schools ended, the Bellamy legacy caused more police-state racism of forced busing that destroyed communities and neighborhoods and deepened hostilities. Those schools still exist. Infants are given social security numbers (socialist slave numbers) that track and tax them for life. Government schools demand the numbers for enrollment.

The practice of placing flags in churches and temples evolved from the "Christian Socialism" and "Military Socialism" of Francis Bellamy, author of the Pledge of Allegiance, the origin of the Nazi salute and Nazi behavior (see the work of the historian Dr. Rex Curry). Inside a mosque, you will not find flags of ISIS, Al-Qaeda, or of terrorist organizations. In government schools, most Muslim students feel that it is not permissible to pledge allegiance to the flag, nor to anything or anyone other than God. But in non-muslim churches and temples you will find the flag of the USA (and memorials to the government traveling around the world killing people).

Bellamy's pledge is different from the Bay`ah (Pledge of Allegiance) in Islam, where a Muslim pledges obedience to the ruler of a region. Bellamy's Bay`ah is recited by little children en masse and every day according to state laws.

The pledge continues as enforced infantilism; adult simpletons chant doggerel written more than a century ago for kindergartners.

How did so many people over the decades write about the USA's Pledge of Allegiance and the swastika and fail to make the discoveries in this book (discoveries that were made by Dr. Curry)? What caused the forgotten history? How could those writers (some of whom viewed historic photographs of the early pledge's Nazi salute), have failed (or refused?) to even ask the questions: (1) Was the Pledge of Allegiance the origin of the Nazi salute and Nazi behavior? (2) Did it impact Germany and other countries at all?

The societal amnesia is the fault of government's schools (socialist schools) that will never ask these questions about the daily pledge ritual and its relationship to socialism in Germany and worldwide. The government's schools have conditioned researchers and writers not to ask or answer the questions that have been answered here.

The word "Nazi" is used to hide the true origin of "Nazi": it means "national socialist." The word "Nazi" evolved from the first two syllables of the German word "national" in the term "national socialist." Hitler did not call himself a "Nazi"; he called himself a "national socialist." Bellamy did not call himself a "Nazi"; he called himself a "national socialist." The word "Nazi" continues to be used to cover up the connections between German socialism and American socialism. Francis Bellamy was a Nazi; he was an American Nazi.

Those are some of the reasons why government schools are unconstitutional: they violate the First Amendment right to freedom of speech and freedom of the press. The government schools (socialist schools) tell everyone what to think and say and write.

And there is a second reason why government schools are unconstitutional: they violate everyone's right to due process of law and to a fair jury trial. Government schools tell everyone to submit to unjust laws, to submit to socialism, and to render verdicts of "guilty."

The Pledge of Allegiance is a fundamental part of the USA's police state. The pledge is a daily Milgram experiment, a witch hunt, and it demonstrates the banality of evil. Litigation continues to occur for persecution of people who refuse.

Fight antidisestablishmentarianism. Please help stop the Pledge of Allegiance and the socialism that it promotes and perpetuates. Remove the pledge from the flag, remove flags from schools, and remove schools from government.

Support the "Stop the Pledge of Allegiance Foundation." And take the pledge not to pledge.

- 15 -

RESEARCH EXPOSING LIBERAL FASCISM

The author Jonah Goldberg in the book "Liberal Fascism: The Secret History of the American Left, From Mussolini to the Politics of Meaning" cites Dr. Rex Curry. The following is an excerpt:

Religion was the glue that held this American national socialism together. Bellamy believed that his brand of socialist nationalism was the true application of Jesus' teachings. His cousin Francis Bellamy, the author of the Pledge of Allegiance, was similarly devoted. A founding member of the first Nationalist Club of Boston and co-founder of the Society of Christian Socialists, Francis wrote a Sermon, "Jesus, the Socialist," that electrified parishes across the country. In an expression of his "military socialism," the Pledge of Allegiance was accompanied by a [stiff-arm] salute to the flag in American public schools. Indeed, some contend that the Nazis got the idea for their salute from America. (page 216).

...The story of the Pledge of Allegiance and its National Socialist roots is a fascinating one. Dr. Rex Curry, a passionate libertarian, has made the issue his white whale. (page 440, n. 25)

The book "From a 'Race of Masters' to a 'Master Race': 1948 to 1848" by the author A. E. Samaan (2013) states:

Dr. Rex Curry, the professor and attorney from Florida, has debated and largely proven the unavoidable evidence that Hitler's National Socialism was significantly influenced by Bellamy's 'nationalistic' form of 'socialism.' Curry is famous for making the claim that Hitler adopted the 'stiff-arm salute' from Francis and Edward Bellamy. (page 589).

Thus, Dr. Curry's claims that much of the fanfare and propaganda we now attribute to the Hitler Youth and the Nuremberg rallies actually originated with American customs, are definitely sound. (Samaan at page 590).

Professor Curry ... has been researching the link between Hitler's National Socialism and Edward Bellamy's 'socialistic' form of 'nationalism.' (Samaan at page 594).

The Sonoran News in Arizona explained the following in an article by Linda Bentley:

....Dr. Rex Curry, a libertarian lawyer who has done vast research on the Pledge's socialist roots, provides pro bono services nationwide to educate students and teachers about 'the right to reject robotic ritualism.' The history of the Pledge simply proves Upham and Ford were able to capitalize on the promotion of Bellamy's socialist agenda, and it's not over yet.

From the Daily Herald, in Provo, Utah, with Randy Wright, the Executive Editor:

Dear Dr. Curry -- Thanks for your help on short notice last night. The subject of the Pledge of Allegiance came up in connection with a rally at a local college in support of the phrase 'under God.' Your material made a terrific sidebar. Little known facts from the past.

From "God Save the South: A Treasure Chest of Forbidden Information," By John Thomas Nall:

The Pledge of Allegiance (1892) was the origin of the raised arm salute adopted later by the National Socialist German Workers Party (Nazis). The Pledge was written by Francis Bellamy, cousin to Edward Bellamy (the author), and both were self-proclaimed national socialists in the United States. The original Pledge began with a military salute that was then extended out toward the flag. In practice, the second gesture was performed palm down. The gesture was not an ancient Roman salute. All of these are discoveries of the symbologist Dr. Rex Curry (author of "Pledge of Allegiance Secrets"). (page 208).

In "Cosmic Evolution: The Accelerated Human," the author James B Lawrence wrote:

...new discoveries show that American soldiers used the swastika as their symbol early in World War I, and up to 1941, against Germany. The symbol was used by Americans in the French Escadrille Lafayette, by the 45th Infantry Division, and on Boeing P-12 planes. The discoveries are in the growing body of work by the historian Dr. Rex Curry (author of 'Swastika Secrets'). He has previously shown how socialists in the USA originated the modern swastika as overlapping 'S' letters for 'Socialists' joining together in a utopian 'Socialist Society.' During the time when American soldiers adopted the swastika, the symbol was associated in the USA with the growing popularity of 'military socialism,' a dogma touted by Edward Bellamy, the American author of the international bestseller 'Looking Backward,' (1887) known as the bible of National Socialism. The symbol was also famous in the USA as alphabetical symbolism for socialism in the Theosophical Society (TS), from 1875. In 1888, the Theosophical Society teamed up with Bellamy's Nationalist movement for military socialism. The 'Bellamy swastika' spread. By 1915, the symbol was

also widely popular as an ornamental 'Good Luck' symbol, as in a 1915 postcard showing the American flag posed favorably with a swastika. (Introduction page ix and in works cited).

Pastor Alvin H Franzmeier: *"...the Sig-Rune became an 'S" and two together became the swastika and represented socialists joining together to form the National Socialist German Workers' party. In 1935 the swastika flag became official for Germany. The swastika symbol was not called that, but rather a HakenKreuz or hooked cross. This was Hitler's attempt to unite the church with the state, especially since German culture was strongly influenced by Christianity. You can find more on these topics on Rex Curry's website and its various pages. He has some interesting things to say about the use of the swastika also in America up to the start of WW II, as well as the open hand salute. The symbol was used by various socialist groups, not only in the USA, but also in the USSR."*

Matt Crypto: *"Before Dr. Curry's work, I had never viewed photographs nor film footage showing the early Nazi salute of the Pledge of Allegiance. At that time, I did not even know that the Nazis were the 'National Socialist German Workers Party' and that they did not refer to themselves as 'Nazis.' I once doubted the greatness of His Excellency Professor Doctor Sir Rex Curry, but he sure put me in my place."*

From Wikipedia: *"The American socialist Francis Bellamy's Pledge of Allegiance to the U.S. flag was the origin of the Nazi salute and Nazi behavior (e.g. robotic chanting to flags) under Hitler's German socialism. German socialists used the Nazi flag's symbol to represent crossed 'S' letters for their socialism (see work of the historian Dr. Rex Curry)."*

Jimmy Wales, Wikipedia's founder, has also commented on the influence of Dr. Curry's work on Wikipedia. The discoveries have been publicized and verified by many readers and writers on Wikipedia.

It is unfortunate that Wikipedia is an anonymous bulletin board that changes by the millisecond. That is because anyone can participate and "anyone" includes Neo-Nazis on Wikipedia who delete historic documentary film footage and other factual material showing Dr. Curry's work (regarding the U.S. as the origin of the notorious stiff-armed gesture via the military salute in the early Pledge of Allegiance; and the swastika as alphabetical symbolism for socialism). Wikipedia is notorious for displaying lies despite the efforts of many other noted historians and writers (including Timothy Messer-Kruse, John Seigenthaler, Philip Roth) to correct the glaring falsehoods.

STOP FASCISM IN THE USA

Once upon a time, there was a brave little boy named "Skippy" who decided to end bullying at his school. All the teachers at Francis Bellamy Elementary School were supportive when Skippy set a date to launch his anti-bullying campaign. He was going to give all the other children fun rubber wristbands colored red, white, and blue with the embossed phrase "Say No to Bullies!" Small American flags on little sticks were similarly embossed. The fun freebies were patterned after the red, white, and blue colors of the large flag painted on their school's exterior, and after the flag waving on the pole in front of their school.

When the big day came, Skippy was at school early in his homeroom class as the teacher began the day with the Pledge of Allegiance. The teacher, Miss Fulford, noticed that Skippy did not stand for the pledge as he always had in the past.

Miss Fulford interrupted the pledge and asked "Skippy, why do you remain seated during the Pledge of

Allegiance?"

In his childish voice, Skippy said, "The Pwedge of Aweegiance is part of my campaign against bulwying. Children think that they have to chant the pwedge. The pwedge is the first bulwying that begins everwy day for wus."

"Do you have some new wacko religious beliefs that have turned you so naughty?" the teacher demanded of Skippy.

"No, Miss Fulford," said Skippy, "I wesearched the histowy. Nazi salutes came from the pwedge!"

"Well, we'll have none of that mister!" the teacher warned, "Even if you won't join everyone else, then you will stand up in respect, and keep your mouth shut!"

There was an awkward pause, as Skippy stared at the teacher, and the teacher glared at Skippy. Miss Fulford realized that Skippy would not move from his seated position. She pointed at the door and screamed, "TO THE PRINCIPAL'S OFFICE!"

Later that day, all the children rejoiced as they helped the school lynch Skippy. His lifeless body was left to hang from the flag pole, underneath the glorious star-spangled banner that Skippy would dishonor never more. As the sun set on Old Glory, the entire school (or rather, what remained of it) chanted the Pledge of Allegiance, as a murder of crows gormandized until they were satiated. Skippy's little feet and hands had been bound with his own kid-sized rubber bracelets that said "Say No To Bullies!"

DEAD WRITERS CLUB

Micky Barnetti is a philologist and a forensic fraud analyst. Barnetti's work (with the assistance of the author Ian Tinny) led to the arrest, trial, conviction, and imprisonment of America's Dumbest Criminals (and the foreclosure of their homes, along with victim restitution liens, and criminal forfeiture judgments, in amounts totaling millions of dollars).

Barnetti collaborates with the Dead Writer's Club ("DWC" -an author's group) and assists the Pointer Institute for Media Studies to provide remedial education to journalists about history, economics, and government.

Matt Crypto is an investigative journalist, free thinker, researcher, and ardent opponent of authoritarianism.

Ian Tinny is a mental health counselor working with the United States Probation Office, federal judges, and various sociopathic criminals in the justice system. He is also a member of the Dead Writers Club.

Other titles by the Dead Writers Club and/or Barnetti include: "Drug Detection Dog Training – Libertarian Lawyers Fight Police State USA," at http://www.amazon.com/dp/1500735280

The self-titled "Dead Writers Club" is available at http://www.amazon.com/dp/150255898X

"BFFs Analects" is available at http://www.amazon.com/dp/1502368781

The groundbreaking book "Pledge of Allegiance & Swastika Secrets" (a semi-biographical work about the nation's leading authority on the Pledge of Allegiance and his many discoveries about its bizarre past and present) from No Pledge Publishing at http://www.amazon.com/dp/148121618X

The DWC also assisted with the following:

A classic science fiction tale revealing an amazing discovery about time travel at http://www.amazon.com/dp/1500588091

The book "World History" at http://www.amazon.com/dp/1511817488

"Lies My Teacher Told Me" is available at http://www.amazon.com/dp/1515248720

A biography of Francis Bellamy at http://www.amazon.com/dp/1515096874

=